FREE ROBUX

freebie.robloxiakid.com/r

An Unofficial Roblox Story

Diary of a Roblox Noob: Jailbreak 2.0

Interactive Diaries

Robloxia Kid

Contents

1   Too Good to be True!   1

2   Time to think about things..   7

3   No one really reads the fine print...   9

4   What's a crappe?   17

5   A Really Strange Dog.   19

6   Solitary Confinement!   25

7   The Great Robux Counterfeiter.   28

8   The coming of.. Boon!   32

9   Meeting the Oculars for the first time!   40

10   What Might Have Been.   46

11   Two Monsters Collide!   49

12   Kings of the Roost.   57

13   Lucky Thirteen: The Name's BOON!   61

14   It's time for a Jailbreak!   65

15   Boon vs PSP! The Big Showdown!   73

16   No Need for Trouble.   78

17   Honor among thieves.   81

18   No one gets left behind.   83

Entry # 1

Too Good to be True!

"This is gorgeous! It's so wonderful!"

I couldn't believe the sight in front of me. I was almost jumping out of my pants, hugging the multi-colored brick walls around me. Okay, let's not do the jumping out of my pants thing... Sorry about that. Well, my eyes were almost popping out of their sockets, and my tongue was wagging like that of a thirsty dog. There, that's more of family-friendly image, eh? Look, let's put it bluntly. The house was AWESOME!!! The sales agent, well, oh-kay.. Not so.

I didn't even know Amed from before. Actually, I only got to see the house because he was so persistent! Otherwise, I would turn to my friend Sally, who also worked as a sales agent. But Amed was so persistent that a noob like me simply couldn't refuse.

"All the furniture is made of expensive oak from the Lumber Tycoon game. These chairs and couches are a dream to sit on! You would be a veritable king once you sat on them. But the price is something even a noob could afford!"

Yeah, I know. Amed was really laying it on me, with all the gravy and mustard. He probably needed the sale just as much as I loved the house and then some, but I didn't really care. I mean, I know when someone's trying to hard-sell me. I used to be a salesman myself, but it didn't really matter now. The house was just awesome, and it blew me away.

"And what's this?"

I pointed at a strange structure that seemed to be made of soft clay or rock. It was the centerpiece of the living room, and any guest would easily see it once he entered the house. The structure did not look like anything I had ever seen and actually looked quite formless.

"Ah that! That's the new rage in all the art and culture circles! That's what you call a crappe!"

"A what? That doesn't seem like a nice word at all!"

"It's a double p! And you forgot the e! The e is pronounced "ey" as in "hey" so you say it like crappey! It's trending everywhere! You have one of this, and you're part of the "IT" crowd. The trendsetters! The social influencers! The big ones, the ones who could say they've made it!"

"Uh what does it do?" I said awkwardly.

"Nothing! It does nothing! That's the beauty of it, don't you think?" Amed said.

"Oh-kay. I guess it does have its appeal.."

Crappe'. With an 'ey.' Okay.. I confess I had no idea what this shmuck was talking about, but if there's anything I don't like, it's looking dumb. So I kinda downplayed my ignorance of the crappe. Besides, if Amed said it was cool and the 'in' thing, then I simply had to have it, right?

"Cool! I'm sure it'll make a great centerpiece for the house. My neighbors will all be so envious of me!"

Amed placed his blocky arm on my shoulder. It was kinda cold and clammy.

"Come on, Noob! You said it yourself. This is a wonderful house! The interior is spacious, comfortable, and it has design values that make you look a lot richer than you actually are. Plus, as you can see the house is right on top of the hill here at Robloxia, and you can see the entire Roblox universe from above. It's a great view, and it's also near a lot of the important games like High School, Work at a Pizza Place, the entire city of Bloxburg and…"

The whole Robloxia looked so cool with the neon lights of the stores, and the cars running around the streets, like little well, toy cars. Everything was so cute, and that was when I saw it. My eyes were attracted to a nice little brown building. It looked so cute because it was the only building without any neon lights, and the drab brown paint actually made it look a little unique. A strange cut above the rest sorta thing.

"What's that place?"

Amed shook his head, and smiled.

"Ah, that's the prison. From the jailbreak game, obviously. Only I heard that there haven't been any jailbreaks in quiet some time there. So I suggest you shouldn't visit it!" he said, with a quick giggle.

"Of course not!" I exclaimed.

"It's a wonderful house, Amed. It really is. And the price seems so reasonable. I can easily get to work at a pizza place from here, like you said. And the view! Wow! This deal seems.."

"Too good to be true? Come on Noob, it's not. It's simply a good deal. Sometimes that's just the way things are in life. Sometimes, good deals are just there, and you simply have to snatch them while they're there."

Amed drove the point really good. I had to give him kudos for being such a solid salesperson. He did have a wonderful home, and I was really that close to buying it. Still, like any good customer, I had my doubts. I didn't just want to fork him all my hard-earned Robux just like that. No way! After all, I still had Sally, and she was also offering me this cheap little house some miles from this place. Honestly, I felt a lot more comfortable getting Sally's place, because I knew her well, and this Amed character seemed a tad shady. And his custom shirt looked way too expensive for a sales agent. Still the house was amazing and seemed to be too good to resist.

All right stop there! This isn't just a regular diary, but an interactive one. Here, you will have to make decisions for Noob so that the story can progress. These choices will appear constantly throughout the story, branching out and leading Noob on different paths and to different fates. In short, Noob will pay for any bungling choices you make, while you sit back in the comfort of your chair, reading this! Pretty cool for you, but not so cool for Noob, eh? So, let's get on with the tough choices!

If you think Noob should buy the house go to Entry #3(page 9)!

If you think that Noob should just take Sally's offer go to Entry #4 (page 17)!

If you think that Noob should think and consider his options a little more, go to Entry #2 (page 7)!

Entry #2:

Time to think about things..

The house looked great and all, but I'm not really the kind of person who did things on impulse. You can understand, right? I mean, after all the Roblox adventures I've been on, life has taught me a lesson: don't rush into things, Noob! The most reasonable thing for good old Noob to do was to weigh his options a little more before making a decision.

"Look Amed. It's a wonderful place. It really is. I think it's more than just great, but I can't just buy the house now. I mean, this is a big purchase and all.."

"And it's the rest of your life we're talking about here in Robloxia. I understand! Go ahead and take your time if you wish, but I'm telling you, you'll never get a better deal like this, anywhere you go."

"I am glad you understand!"

"Of course, of course! Take all the time you need! I'll be waiting. Then again, don't take your time! Someone less nooby than you might just take the house before you come to your senses.

Yep, that was Amed for you. He was really trying to push me to get the house, but I couldn't budge. I mean, I wasn't just buying a new custom shirt here! This was something I had to think about, and think hard.

Okay, so I returned to my small and cramped apartment, and I immediately began to regret not getting the house from Amed. I mean, staying in that cramped place after seeing such a wonderful house can do that to you. Think about it, after all the adventures I've been on, I don't want to end up here!

"Man, maybe I should have gotten the house already! But Sally's is much cheaper, and I know Sally well, even if her house isn't as amazing as Amed's. Oh man, what am I going to do?"

I was really torn with my choices. I only knew that I couldn't live in this small, cramped apartment any longer. So what was I supposed to do? Oh yeah, I forgot! This is an interactive diary, right? That's what you're there for! You tell me what to do!

If you think Noob should buy the house go to Entry #3 (page 9)!

If you think that Noob should just take Sally's offer go to Entry #4 (page 17)!

No one really reads the fine print...

I really thought that I should think long and hard about what to do. Thinking long and hard meant only one thing. Meditation, breathing exercises, time to be alone? Jogging in the park, taking a swim, or some exercise to put me in a good mood? Maybe even listening to relaxing music before going to bed to sleep on the decision? Nah. I did what I always do when I'm making a big decision.

Order pizza! Yeah! I ordered the quadruple-layer, super family size with all the toppings pizza!!! Boy, did it taste great! All that cheese and toppings was simply food for the soul. Absolutely heavenly. It only took me ten minutes and several burps to come to a decision.

Amed was waiting triumphantly for me on the house's front porch. He extended his arms towards me in welcome. He could definitely smell the sale now!

"Noob! So glad you came back! I guess you've made up your mind?"

"Definitely! I've decided to get the house!"

Amed jumped for joy on the spot and did a fist pump.

"Oh yeah! Got the sale!"

Yep, I saw that fist pump.

"Uhm, aren't you a bit too well, enthusiastic about this sale?"

"Oh no, no! You misunderstand! I'm simply so happy that I've provided another happy customer with his dream home! This is a wonderful job, I tell you! I just love helping people!"

"Ah, well it is a good house. I'm glad you were able to show it to me."

"Only too happy to help, Mr. Noob."

Okay, so maybe it was a little suspicious that Amed did a fist pump and just jumped for joy when I agreed to buy the house. I mean, he was a salesman, after all, but he did seem a little too happy... Whatever the case was, at least he called me *Mr. Noob*. And no one ever does that!

I didn't give it any more thought and decided to go ahead with the sale. So, I plunked in the cold, hard Robux and handed it to Amed, who was only too eager to accept. I couldn't help but notice the way he jumped for joy at the sale, and how enthusiastically he took the money. Oh well, perhaps now he could afford a house of his own!

We signed a lot of papers with a lot of fine print and small letters. A lot of boring stuff to scroll down through. Yada, yada, yada, legal stuff yada, yada. Blah, blah, blah, more legal stuff, blah, blah, blah. Yeah, I didn't even bother to read most of the contract. I mean, who really reads that stuff? Do you read all the *Terms and Conditions*, and *Privacy Policy* notifications anyway? Seriously, no one does! You just click "Agree".

Once Amed was gone, and I was finished paying and signing the right papers, I immediately made myself at home in his new surroundings. I fixed myself a nice cheese sandwich and some milk. I also prepared some Roblox chocolate cookies for desert. Everything was neat and ready to eat.

"Ah my first meal in my great new home!"

I snickered as I took one Roblox cookie and bit at it. Yummy! Okay, I confess, I have a strange habit of eating some dessert first before the actual meal. It's not advisable, I know, but hey, I'm a big boy now, and I can do pretty much whatever I want. But don't be jealous! Your day will come too. For now, just be happy for old Noob here. After all, I am in my brand new all awesome house! One that has a crappe in it! I bet yours doesn't!

I was about to chew on the cookie some more when the most unexpected thing happened. I was shocked out of my mind when the front door was kicked in. Several special ops cops who must have been from the Phantom Forces game entered the house, and they all pointed their weapons at me!

"What on Earth is going on?"

"Hands on your head! Now!"

The cops kept their guns pointed at me, and I was scared out of my mind! I had no choice but to just keep my hands up, like they said.

"Okay, okay! Take it easy! What are you guys doing in my house, anyway?"

None of them answered me, and instead, I felt a pair of cuffs get slapped on my wrist. After they slapped the cuffs on, one of the cops kicked me from behind, and knocked me to the ground.

"Ouch! That stings!"

"Stay down! You're going straight to the slammer for what you've done!"

I felt several arms pinning him down to the ground. This was probably how a roach that got stepped on felt like.

"That's what I've been asking you guys! Why are you arresting me? I've done nothing wrong?"

One of the cops chuckled behind me.

"You've got a lot of nerve to act all smug and clean down there!"

"What are you talking about? I've never committed a crime in my life!"

"Really now? If that's the case, then what's that huge chunk of rock doing in your house?"

The cop pointed at the crappe that Amed had been talking about earlier.

"That thing? Can't you see it's just a conversation piece! A centerpiece for the living room!"

"You really want to keep up this dumb act of yours? Can't you see it's not just a hunk of rock? It's something else entirely!"

"I don't understand what you're talking about!"

"Fine. Does this help?"

The cop pushed the piece of rock down, and it tumbled to the ground. It shattered once it fell, revealing large chunks of Robux coins. There was easily a fortune inside!

"Robux! I never knew there was money inside!"

"Not just any kind of money. Counterfeit Robux! We've been trying to track down the stuff for so long! We finally managed to find it here in your new home!"

Counterfeit Robux in my home? I just couldn't believe what I was hearing. It all sounded like some bad dream, and a part of me still refused to believe that this was all happening. I stared at the shattered remains of the crappe, and it suddenly looked a lot less attractive than it did before.

"I didn't know that that thing there was illegal! I just bought this house today from a salesman named Amed and.."

"Shut up already! You can explain all of that to a judge when your hearing starts! In the meantime, you're going straight to jail!"

"No! I can prove it! I've got a contract and a deed of sale that I signed only a few hours ago! It proves that I bought this house from that creepy salesman Amed, and he tricked me!"

"You mean this deed of sale?"

One of the cops took out a piece of paper. I recognized it as the one I signed earlier, and my heart was suddenly full of hope.

"Yeah! Yeah, that's the one! I signed that earlier! My signature's there!"

"Exactly. It says here;"

"I Noob, of sound mind and body do hereby admit to having freely stashed and hid away a million RS worth of counterfeit Robux. I hid them in the crappe' which is really just a rock to make me look cool. I admit that I love the life of a smuggler and counterfeiter. It has always been my dream to be a thief, a scoundrel, a rogue and.."

"Wait, wait, wait! That doesn't sound right! That's not the contract I signed earlier! It can't be!"

"It's your signature right here!"

The cop showed me my signature, and I recognized the paper now. Now I could see what all that blah, blah, blah really was. If only I actually did read the fine print. But no one really does read that stuff..

It finally dawned on me. I should have definitely bought Sally's house.

It sure looks bad for Noob now, but don't worry! This is definitely not the end of his adventures! In fact, this is where it really starts to take off! Just remember to make the right choice when the chance comes! Noob's fate depends on you!

Go to Entry #5 (page 19) to see what happens next!

Entry #4:

What's a crappe?

It was a tough choice, but I decided to go with Sally's offer. It was not easy pulling myself away from the wonderful house that Amed offered, but I just decided that it was more practical to go with Sally. After all, I knew her from way back, and her house was a lot cheaper.

"You made the right choice, Noob." Sally said.

I looked around. Sally's house was a lot smaller than Amed's place, but it was still much bigger than my tight apartment. That was still a good thing, and it was a lot more affordable. Besides, I guess I really couldn't trust Amed. There was something off about that guy, I just wasn't sure what it was.

"I think I did, Sally. I think I did."

"You don't sound too convinced, Noob. Come on! You know me. I wouldn't give you a bad deal. You just met that Amed character. I know I shouldn't say bad things about the competition, but that guy has no track record. We don't know him from the first Roblox player. He may have had a good deal but something seemed off about it, if you ask me."

"You think something was off about him?"

"I don't know, but if you ask me, maybe. There was something that wasn't right about that house. I just couldn't place it."

I took a look at the house again. It was all nice, and everything was in order but something was missing. Something that Amed's house had.

"Where's the crappe? The house doesn't have a crappe?"

Sally gave me a really strange look.

"What is a crappe?"

Well, that was the end of that. I got the house, got a job at the pizza place and even got a nice dog later on. Everything was cool and fine, but nothing amazing. What happened? Life went on, and maybe that was for the best. Still, I couldn't shake that feeling from the back of my mind that I had dodged a bullet, or that I might have had some amazing adventure if I took the other house. Oh well, never mind. It was just a feeling anyway.

The End

Pretty anti-climactic ending eh? Don't worry! There are a lot more better endings you can get! Double back and keep reading to get the many other endings you may have missed!

Entry #5:

A Really Strange Dog.

The cops whisked me out of the house and tossed me into an armored car. The cuffs were still tightly on my wrists, and it made them ache.

"An armored car? Come on boys! I'm no dangerous fugitive!" Noob said.

"Says the guy who smuggled a whole chunk of counterfeit Robux into the suburbs! What you did breaks the universal law of Robloxia, which means that you'd be a fugitive in any Roblox game you visit. You're going away for a very long time, mister!"

"Universal law? Going away for a very long time? Oh boy, this is isn't real! This isn't happening to me! I thought you said I could appeal my case or explain it to the courts!"

They all laughed at me inside the van. These guys really thought I was lower than trash or something.

"Yeah, I said that, didn't I? You can appeal your case, when the judge schedules a hearing for you. That could take around twenty updates at best. Forty at worst. And if the judge finds you guilty of counterfeiting that Robux, well, you could stay in the slammer for the rest of your life!"

"What?"

I couldn't believe anything that I was hearing now. None of that sounded very nice, and I desperately wanted to get out of the armored van. If only I wasn't so stupid and impulsive! I should have known better than to get a house from that shady Amed character! If I had just bought the house Sally was offering none of this would have happened. Now, it was simply too late for any regrets. I was facing real, hard time for a crime I did not even commit. This was terrible. In fact, this was beyond terrible!

The elite forces squad brought me to a very familiar building. I recognized it immediately by its brown and cream paint. Yeah, it was that building. It was the jail that I noticed from my dream house. It was the same jail that Amed joked about with me. Well, it looked like I was going to get a closer, more personal view of it now.

"All right, Noob! Get out of the armored car, now!"

I felt the cop's boot on my butt. I was kicked out of the armored car, as the back doors swung open. I landed right on the grounds of the notorious Jailbreak server, and the landing was anything but comfortable.

"Owtch! Couldn't you guys take it easy, for once? You've already got me!"

"A prisoner like you has no rights! Now get up, and get in jail already!"

One of the cops picked me up like a rag doll from the ground. Then he led me into the jail where a large man in uniform was waiting for me. Beside the large man was a large dog, who appeared shaven from the head down. I could tell that the dog had been shaved because there were patches of fur at the ends of his legs to create the appearance of fluffy cuffs. The dog stared at me, but didn't growl or bark back. That came as something of a relief, as the dog seemed pretty large, and was held back only by a thin chain.

"We got a new one for you, Mack!" one of the swat cops told the man.

The large man grinned at Noob.

"So what did you do to get thrown in here?"

"I didn't do anything! Nice dog by the way." I said.

"This one's in a bit of denial, Warden Mack! He keeps insisting that he didn't do anything, even if we found a large chunk of rock with counterfeit Robux in his house!"

Mack scowled at Noob. For a moment, I thought that he looked just like his dog.

"You kept counterfeit Robux in your house? That's bad stuff, boy! Looks like you're going to be staying here for long! It's off to maximum security with you!"

All right. That really sounded very welcoming and friendly. Not.

"I didn't do any of that! I just bought the house and.."

"You didn't do none of that stuff, even if we've got a signed paper here, stating that you did do all that stuff and you willingly and gleefully admitted to doing all of that!"

The warden flashed the contract in my face again. I was really beginning to regret not reading the fine print.

"I didn't read the fine print! Come on, warden! No one reads the fine print, right? I mean, you don't really read that stuff before you play a game, right? It was the same thing here! Cut me some slack already!"

"Whatever! Come with me. It's time to meet your fellow inmates. I trust you'll get along with them quite nicely."

The way Warden Mack said that didn't do me any favors. Something told me that I would not get along with anybody in this place.

It didn't take long for Warden Mack to show me my new cell. It was a small cell that was even more cramped than my old apartment ever was. There were two beds attached to the wall, that made the cell even more cramped, and a tall and lean inmate who seemed indifferent to me. He didn't look mean, but he didn't look like he cared much for me, either. Somehow, a sink and toilet was squeezed into the small cell, making it almost impossible to move around.

"All right, get in!" the warden said.

"I'm supposed to be staying in there?"

"Get in, or deal with the dog."

Deal with the dog, eh? Well, that didn't seem like a bad proposition. After all, he had a lumpy, face with sad, droopy eyes. With his furry cuffs, he looked anything but threatening. I mean, how bad could he be, right? I'd just pet him a bit and he'd love me.

If you think that Noob should refuse to enter his cell go to Entry #6 (page 25)!

If you think that Noob should simply just follow the warden's order, go to Entry #7 (page 28)!

Entry #6:

Solitary Confinement!

"I'm not going in there!"

I guess it was a little cocky, but I decided to defy the warden's order. After all, what could a cuddly teddy bear like that dog of his do? It just looked so huggable and non-threatening..

"So you think you can just refuse a direct order like that, eh? Go get him, Mack Jr!"

"Wait a minute? Mack Jr? What kind of name is.."

Before I could even think of how strange the name of that dog sounded, the dog was on top of me. When the warden let go of the chain, he moved like lightning. That large tummy of his and cute appearance was really deceiving, and he was on top of me, almost instantly.

"Great! This huge dog is going to bite off my face! What was I even thinking doing that? I'm done for!"

I could feel the warm, moist breath of the dog on me, and there was really nothing I could do now. I just covered my face with my arms and hoped for the best, which wasn't really much. That was when a strange thing happened.

"Who did this to you? Who did this to you? Who did this to you?"

From the moment I entered the prison, the big dog never made a single sound. He just kinda looked at everyone funny like. Now that he was on top of me, I expected him to growl before ripping my face off. Instead, he kept repeating that phrase over and over again, like a parrot or something. He also had a very nice, calming voice. I must say, Mack Jr. would have made a great singer if could only say something more than just that.

"What's happening?" I exclaimed in surprise.

"Who did this to you?"

The dog continued to repeat the phrase, without even thinking. Yeah, I guess that was the dog's version of a bark.

"Think you can get away with refusing my orders around here, eh? My fearsome dog ought should make you think twice about doing anything funny again!"

"Uh, he sure is fearsome, warden."

"Get up!"

The warden tugged at the chain, and Mack Jr backed off. Despite his strange bark, the dog seemed poised and ready to bite me, at a moment's notice.

"You think you can act all cocky in this jail? My jail? No way! Come with me!"

Two more guards came from out of nowhere, and picked me up. They led me out of the general population area and somewhere which seemed much more quiet. It was a long and dark corridor with only a single door at the end. There was an eerie quiet in the area which was very creepy.

"What is this place?"

"Solitary confinement. This is what you get for defying the warden and his dog" – one of the guards said, pointing to the door that was now being unlocked by the warden.

The room was nothing but a small space that was the smallest of all. There was nothing and no one inside and it was also very dark. It would not be a very nice place to stay in, to say the least.

"I'm staying in there? All by myself? No way!" Noob said.

"You're staying in there by yourself for five updates! That should soften you up! Oh, by the way, you don't have a choice! Get him inside, boys!"

I was tossed into the small room, and before he could do anything, the door was locked shut from behind me. Once it was shut, there was barely any light inside the room to see anything. The room was also too small to do anything but just stand or sit. I immediately felt a crushing feeling of being alone in the darkness.

"No! No! Don't leave me here!"

I pounded away at the door, but the guards ignored me. I realized that I was all alone in the room. I was really all alone with nothing but the darkness. I didn't know if I could take this for the entire five updates!

"No! Someone get me out of here!"

No one answered my pleas. Something in the back of my head told me that this was a turning point in my story. I had entered a point of no return, and I was bound to change. Being alone and in the dark like that gave me no choice but to change. Whether it would be for the good or for the bad was still not sure.

Well, it sure looks like Noob has crossed a line here! Solitary confinement promises to change our hero, but like he said, will it be for the better, or for the worse? This is where Noob's fate takes a unique turn, and it's all up to you!

To check out the all-new, all different Noob, and continue the adventure go to Entry #8 (page 32)!

Entry #7:

The Great Robux Counterfeiter.

"Okay, okay, I'm going inside! There's no need to get pushy about it!" Noob said.

I entered the cell without much protest after that. The warden smiled at me. I wasn't about to my chances with that dog of his, no matter how cuddly it looked.

"Good thing you entered the cell quietly. A part of me thought that you would try something stupid. I actually wanted you to do something stupid so I could sick Mack Jr. here on you."

"No way, no way! I'm not about to challenge that dog of yours, warden. He may look all cuddly, cute, and doesn't even bark, but something tells me that there's something different about your dog. Something unpleasant."

The warden nodded.

"He's only unpleasant to strangers and inmates who like to break the rules. You keep your nose clean like that, and we'll have nothing to worry about."

The warden slid the prison door shut from there, and walked away, leaving me all alone with my new cellmate. He seemed quiet and harmless enough, but I kept my guard up. This was after all prison, and I really could not be sure about anything or anyone here.

"Kept your distance from Mack Jr, eh? That was smart. I heard that you wouldn't want to make him, or the warden angry at all."

He was a tall and thin fellow. He had quite the long arms and legs and looked something like one of those circus performers on stilts. Because of his height – unusual for a Roblox character, he had a hard time fitting into the cell which had a low ceiling. The inmate had to crouch all the time, when he stood up inside.

"Yeah, I figured as much. A dog like that, that doesn't say anything can't be as harmless as it looks. Name's Noob by the way."

"Carlos. Carlos Edasis. I used to study at Roblox High School, not far from here."

Carlos stretched out his hand to me and I shook it.

"Nice to meet you, Carlos. Roblox high school? Isn't it being renovated? I mean it was damaged in some kind of fire, right?"

"Yeah. I was the one who set it on fire, right after I tossed some pie in my teacher's face."

"Who-hoa."

I smiled nervously at Carlos. He seemed so friendly and timid, but it turned out that I was confined with a hardened criminal! The way Carlos described his crimes was also pretty creepy. He mentioned burning his school down, as casually as someone would describe popping a sandwich in a microwave oven.

"How about you, Noob? What did they stick you in here for?"

Noob shook his head.

"Nothing special. They just found this strange rock in my new house. Turns out it was full of counterfeit Robux and.."

"Counterfeit Robux! You're a Robux smuggler! And a counterfeiter too!"

"Well, not exactly. You see.."

"Whoa! You're a genuine smuggler and counterfeiter! I've got a real criminal multi-tasker as my cellmate!"

"What? Listen, I'm not a smuggler, not a counterfeiter or anything like that! Carlos. It was.."

I tried to explain the real circumstances behind my arrest, but it simply didn't matter to Carlos anymore. He simply wouldn't hear any of it. In his mind, I was some great and daring criminal mastermind and that was that. I was a what did he call it? A criminal multi-tasker! I didn't even know how to cook an omelet properly, and now I'm a criminal multi-tasker? This was all just getting out of hand, really quickly, and all because I bought a dream house.

"Look, Noob! You're the real thing! You're a Robux smuggler! I'm not surprised they would try to keep you here! They must be really worried about you, and what you can do!"

"What I can do? But I can't even tie my laces right sometimes!"

"Heh. A real modest joe, eh? I like that. A real man doesn't need to show off his skills until they're absolutely necessary, eh? I like you Noob! I like you, a lot!"

"Oh-kay.."

"I like you so much that I'm going to let you in on a little secret. We're planning an break from this dumb jail that Warden Mack runs! We're going to get out of here, and you can join us! We sure could use a great counterfeit Robux smuggler like yourself! What do you say?"

Carlos' offer was more than tempting, it was screaming at me! Talk about something in your face! I had only been in this place for all of a few minutes, and

I already didn't like it much. I didn't really relish the idea of staying here for years just to wait for my first hearing about a crime I didn't even commit!

By the time they actually found me innocent, the best years of my life may have already passed me by.

No, I did not want that at all for myself.

On the other hand, I also didn't feel too comfortable taking Carlos offer. Carlos referred to me as this great 'criminal multi-tasker' – something I was anything but. If I joined their jailbreak, and they somehow discovered I wasn't who they thought I was, then it could turn out really badly for yours truly. It was time to decide, or rather time for you to decide...

up! This whole thing with you deciding my fate is just downright tough and unfair! I should be the one deciding my fate, but there's nothing I can do, so choose wisely, or else!

If you decide that it's time for Noob to join Carlos' jailbreak go to Entry #9 (page 40)!

If you think that it's simply too risky for Noob to join in jailbreak go to Entry #10 (page 46)!

Entry #8:

The coming of.. Boon!

"All right! Time to go! Solitary confinement's done! You can go out now!"

When the guard opened the door of the cell in solitary confinement, the light rushed to my eyes. It took me a moment to adjust to the sudden lighting, and I had to cover my eyes with my arms. Or maybe I should say biceps. Or maybe I should say pythons. Or maybe I should say pistons. Or maybe I should say.. well, you get the point.

"Whoa, there! Looks like you packed a little extra muscle since they locked you up. You're going to have to squeeze through the door space," the guard said.

"I'll manage."

I saw the look of surprise in the guard's eyes as he saw me, and I couldn't help but grin and chuckle a bit. I guess it was amazing that I had suddenly put on so much weight, and not just weight, but muscle. My whole body was packed with muscle. I had so much muscles all over that I was hunched and crouching from all the muscles my body was packing. Yep, I was now a walking tank. It's a wonder what a little alone time can do, if you make the most of it.

"How'd you get so uhm, beefy?" the cop asked.

There was more than a hint of tension in his voice.

"Pushups will do wonders for you. You should try it sometime." Noob said.

"Uh ok.. I'll keep that in mind."

Looking at the guard, I could almost read his mind. I knew what he was thinking.

"His anger and frustration must have combined with his being alone for so long, to create this monster!"

I noticed how the guard kept his hand close to his baton. He also kept wiping sweat from his brow, as he kept glancing at me. Heh, he was really worried that I would try to do something to him. I actually thought he might just embarrass himself and wet himself from sheer fear. Okay, sorry about that. Maybe I shouldn't have said that. This is after all, a family friendly interactive diary, so blot that out. He was just scared out of his mind, but he didn't really have to be. The guard should have realized that he had nothing to fear from me at all. It was someone else who should have been shaking in his boots, once he saw me.

"Oh-ho, ho! Look who's been working out!" the warden said.

"Pushups. You should try it sometime. Instead of eating donuts and cheeseburgers."

Oh yeah, baby. It was a direct challenge all right. I hurled my words straight at the warden like a lightning bolt. He took it pretty well, but I could tell that he and that ridiculous dog of his kinda shivered and tensed up, even just a little when I said that. I could even hear the murmurs everywhere after I spoke.

"Oh no. It's going to happen now. Warden Mack isn't going to take such a comment lying down."

I think the other guards really thought that some kind of violence would erupt right then and there. Honestly, I did too, and I couldn't wait. I wanted to test out my new bod, and hit something, preferably the warden's blocky face. Unfortunately, the warden disappointed me, and didn't do anything stupid at all.

"Yeah, maybe I will try it sometime. You know what they say about wisdom. You can get it, even from the most unlikeliest of sources."

I guess Warden Mack wasn't as dumb as he looked.

"I'll be going back into my cell now. You better just run along Warden." I said.

I entered my cell, and basically, the warden and the guards just let me be. There was no big fight. Not yet, at least. That was when he said it.

"I'll be watching you Noob. You better not try anything stupid again, or you'll be getting a lot worse than just solitary."

I heard him say that name. That wasn't my name anymore. It was someone else from a long time ago. Now, I was different. Now, I was better.

"Don't call me Noob anymore. From now on, it's Boon!"

The warden smiled and nodded.

"Sure thing. **BOON.**"

The warden left, but it was clear that a storm was brewing. This was clearly far from over.

"Whoa. That was intense dude. I've never seen anyone stare down the warden like that. Are you asking for trouble, dude?"

I glanced at my new cellmate. I had never really gotten a good look at him until now. He was a tall and thin fellow. He had quite the long arms and legs and looked something like one of those circus performers on stilts. Because of his height, he had a hard time fitting into the cell which had a low ceiling. The inmate had to crouch all the time, when he stood up inside.

"Trouble seems to always find me."

The tall, thin man nodded tensely. He clearly wanted to stay on my good side. Smart guy.

"That's life in jail for you, dude. Name's Carlos by the way. Carlos Edasis. I used to study at Roblox High School, not far from here."

"The school that they're renovating because it caught fire?"

"That's the one. I was the one who set it on fire, right after I tossed some pie in my teacher's face."

Carlos was clearly trying to sound cocky and impressive, but I didn't really care. Maybe the old me would have been afraid of him, or would have been shocked about his crimes. Me now? I didn't really care. I knew I could handle anything Carlos would try to throw at me.

"Man that was just cold! You're not impressed? What did you do to get yourself all locked up in here?"

"That's none of your concern, kid. I would appreciate it if you just let me do my thing. You mind your business, and I'll mind my own."

Carlos whistled.

"Man, you are a really cool customer, you know that? Well, that's ok. I actually respect that. I respect it so much, that I'm willing to give you a chance. A real golden opportunity."

"A chance? What are you talking about?"

Carlos was starting to get a little annoying.

"A chance to join my gang!"

"Your gang?"

"Yeah! Think about it, big guy! It would be to your advantage to join a gang in here! After all, this is prison. It isn't easy surviving on your own, no matter how big you are."

"That's exactly why you shouldn't join Carlos' gang of wusses!"

The voice came from the opposite cell. I leaned close to the cell door to hear the voice better.

"Who was that?" I asked.

"Hey! Don't go telling my new friend all sorts of nonsense Hoyce! He's with us, the Oculars!"

"He ain't with anyone, until he's made up his mind! Yeah, you heard me right, big man! I'm offering you an alternative! Carlos and his gang, the Oculars, are the worst gang in jail! Ain't no one respects those boys! You join them, and you'll be laughed out of the joint! If you join us, you join a real gang, with real power! You join us, the T'recsz, you'll have a real chance of being someone in jail. Heh, I saw the way you stared down the warden, big man. If you ask me, you've got the makings of becoming top dog in the entire jail! Join us, and that might even happen."

Carlos poked my arm and went closer to whisper something to me.

"Don't listen to Hoyce, man! I admit, his gang is really tough, probably the toughest gang in the entire prison, but we've got something those big dogs don't have! We've got something none of the gangs are ever going to have!"

I saw Carlos' eyes light up like Christmas lights. He was clearly hiding something, something he believed was of real value.

"What's that?"

Carlos shook his head.

"Ah-ah, big man! I'll only tell you if you join us! So what's it going to be, the Oculars, or T'recsz? The choice is yours, Boon."

Noob, or Boon is facing another tough choice. Yikes! Don't tell him I called him Noob again, or Boon would be really, really mad!

If you think Boon should join the Oculars go to Entry #11 (page 49)!

If you think that Boon should join the T'recsz go to Entry #12 (page 57)!

If you think he should not even join any gang, and simply go solo, go to lucky Entry #13 (page 61)!

Meeting the Oculars for the first time!

"If you're breaking out of this dump, I'm in!"

All right. That really came out better than even I expected. I didn't know I could be that confident and brave, but I guess I simply couldn't stand it in jail anymore. I still wasn't sure if Carlos, and whoever were trying to pull this escape off were trustworthy, or not. It was probably a huge risk too, but either way, I didn't want to rot in jail forever. If there was even a chance to escape, I just had to take it.

"Good man! I knew I could count on you, Noob! Tomorrow, during yard time, I'll introduce you to my other gang mates."

"Other gang mates?"

Carlos nodded.

"Yeah. You didn't think I was going to pull this thing off by myself, did you? If we're even going to have a chance to get out of this stinkhole, we'll need the help of other people. People we can trust. That's why tomorrow, I'm making you an official member of the Oculars, my gang."

The night passed without any incident. I managed to get some sleep and dream about pizza! Yeah, I still love cheesy pizza, even if it was probably that stuff that got me into this mess to begin with. What can I say? Comfort food dies hard!

The morning came, and Yard Time was up. Yard Time was the time when all the prisoners were allowed to spend well, time outside at the prison yard. It was probably the only time anyone could get to go outside the prison.

"Hey guys! I've got us a new member in the gang! Everybody meet Noob!"

Carlos introduced me to two inmates standing in one corner of the large prison yard. One of them looked large and imposing with a big body that seemed to span the corner they were meeting on.

"New guy? Come on, Carlos! We don't need no new guy to get in on the gang!"

"Yeah if he's a member of the gang, that means that he's in on the jailbreak, right?"

Honestly, the two inmates didn't look too pleased to meet me. One was a giant who had purple skin, and one was a little guy with a lot of pimples on his face.

"That's Enzo and Purple Stretchy Pants, by the way. I think you know who's who already, just by looking at them." Carlos said.

"Purple Stretchy Pants? But he's just one giant in purple. He's got no pants on him.." I said.

Then it happened. Before I could react, Purple Stretchy Pants grabbed me by the prison shirt and hoisted me up with one hand. I squirmed in his grip like a worm on a fish hook. I also felt more like a human rag doll on a coat hanger. Either way, it was anything but comfortable being in the grip of Purple Stretchy Pants.

"I'm wearing purple pants. It's not my fault my skin's purple too. Unless you want to make something of it."

"N.. no.. no sir.."

"Put him down PSP! He's a Criminal Multi-tasker!"

"A Criminal Multi-tasker? For real?"

There it was again. Upon hearing the words 'Criminal Multi-tasker,' Enzo and PSP seemed to immediately have a change of heart. It was almost like some kind of magic phrase to give me instant respect, but it kinda creeped me out. I was suddenly and gently put back down.

"Whoa. I've always heard stories about criminal multi-taskers. They say you need to be a different breed of player to be a criminal multi-tasker. They say you got to have drive, focus, and the ability to do ten criminal acts all at once! I always wanted to do that, but I guess I never really developed the stones for it. I mean, I'm really a simple guy at heart."

"No problem. Heh, no hard feelings." I said.

It was still unnerving to see a huge man like PSP turn as meek as a lamb like that, but I decided to just enjoy the moment. After all, the alternative was not so good, right?

"Sorry about being so rough earlier. You can call me PSP for short, by the way. I mean 'Purple, Stretchy, Pants' seems so long, don'cha think?"

"Heh. Yeah, I guess it is pretty long when you think of it", I said nervously.

I was relieved that the gang suddenly respected me for being some bigshot smuggler. But I also began to wonder how long I could keep this story up. The truth of the matter was that I was anything but a Robux Smuggler, or a counterfeiter, for that matter. And I didn't want to face an angry PSP who had realized he was lied to.

"PSP's right. It takes a different breed of player to do what you do. Sorry about the rocky introduction earlier. No hard feelings?"

Enzo stretched out his hand, and I shook it. It didn't matter that I was no criminal multi-tasker now. I simply had to keep appearances going.

"Forget it. What's important is that we break out of this place."

"I'm glad we're all finally on the same page now. Well, let's get down to the nitty-gritty of it then, shall we?"

"Ain't nobody listening, right?"

"Relax Enzo. We can talk. Everyone's all doing their thing, and no one can hear us here. So here's the plan, Noob. Listen up."

"I'm all ears."

Carlos flashed a small item in his pants pocket. He took out only a small portion of the object, just so Noob could get a glimpse of it. He didn't risk taking it out in the open, for fear of any guard or inmate spotting it.

"What's that? Is that a fork?" Noob asked.

Carlos nodded.

"Yep. That's a fork all right, and it's going to be the key to getting us out of here."

Noob couldn't believe any of this.

"A fork? How is a fork going to help us break out of this place? It's a jail full of guards and dogs and everything else to keep us inside!" Noob said.

Carlos smiled at me.

"Have a little faith, Noob. This is how it's going to go down.."

To see how the plan goes down for real continue reading at Entry #14(page 65)!

Entry #10:

What Might Have Been.

"Look, Carlos. I'm sorry, but I don't want to get involved in any shady business. Warden Mack looks like a real tough customer, and I wouldn't want to get on his bad side. I'm not going to stop you or anything, and I won't even tell Mack. Don't worry. I promise. I just don't want to get involved in any of this."

I told Carlos as gently and nicely as I could that I simply would not be a part of any jailbreak. I didn't want to stay in jail for any stretch, especially considering that I didn't really commit a crime. I also didn't want to make my stay any worse than it had to be. I guess I really just got tired of any more exciting stuff in my already messed up situation.

Carlos nodded and smiled. There was clearly a look of disappointment in his face.

"I have to admit, I'm a little disappointed that you would refuse my offer, considering that you're a Criminal multi-tasker and all. I thought that you would have more guts than that. After all, you did counterfeit Robux and all."

"How many times do I have to tell you? I didn't do any of that! I'm innocent!"

Carlos just ignored me, and I eventually just decided to get some sleep.

The morning came, and I woke up to an empty cell. Carlos was nowhere to be found. There were alarm sirens blasting the air, and Warden Mack stood over me as I lay on the bed.

"What on Earth happened here, Noob?" Mack demanded.

"What's going on, Warden? I don't understand what's happening."

"You don't understand, eh? Well, just look at the wall!"

I looked at the wall where the warden was pointing at. There was a huge, gaping hole. Mack Jr was barking at the hole too, or was he?

"Who did this to you? Who did this to you? Who did this to you?"

"Uh, warden. Your dog, he.."

"What? I like the way he barks! Got a problem with it?"

"No sir. Not at all!"

"What happened with Carlos last night?"

"I don't know! I really don't, I swear! I was just sleeping last night. I'm as clueless as you are!"

The warden growled at me. He growled a lot meaner and louder than his dog did. Actually Mack Jr had a soothing kind of voice.

"You better hope you really had nothing to do with this! Because if I find out you helped him in any way, you'll really wish you had just told me!"

"I'm clean, warden! Honest!"

"We'll talk about this later! Guards! We have escaped convicts!"

Warden Mack left me there in my cell to chase Carlos' gang. I thought about that for a while.

"I'll never meet any of them. Probably never get the chance to get out of here like that again.."

I kept thinking about the gang, and the chance that Carlos offered me to escape. The more I thought about it, the more I started to wonder. Did I make the wrong choice?

I guess I would find out in twenty to forty updates. That was when my hearing was up. No, that didn't really sound very comforting at all..

The End.

Yep, I know what you're thinking. That's not the kind of ending you would have wanted, right? So keep reading to get the other better endings!

Entry #11:

Two Monsters Collide!

I smiled at Carlos and winked at him.

"So this gang is the worst in the prison, eh? The one with the least respect? Well, I guess it's time to make it a lot more respectable then. I'm joining the Oculars!"

"Boo-yeah! That's what I'm talking about!"

Carlos looked really pleased at this, and why shouldn't he? I was joining their gang! He raised his palm and gave me a crisp high-five, and promptly paid for it. His palm met mine and it was like slapping a brick wall.

"Owtch! Not so smart to do that.. ouch.." Carlos whimpered.

"Sorry about that, Carlos. I did just get really big, and really strong. Really fast. Sorry.."

"You're making a big mistake, Boon! You ain't going nowhere with a gang like the Oculars! You should've joined us!"

"I'll take that chance."

Hoyce didn't say anything about the matter after that, and poor Carlos had to spend the night trying to sleep with a semi-busted hand.

The morning came soon enough, and all the inmates were led outside for some yard time. This was the best time to meet the other members of Carlos' gang.

"Hey guys! I've got us a new member in the gang! Everybody meet Boon!"

Carlos introduced me to two inmates standing in one corner of the large prison yard. One of them looked large and imposing with a big body that seemed to span the corner they were meeting on.

"New guy? Come on, Carlos! We don't need no new guy to get in on the gang!"

"Yeah if he's a member of the gang that means, that he's in on the jailbreak, right?"

The two inmates did not look pleased to meet me. One was a giant who had purple skin, and one was a little guy with a lot of pimples on his face.

"That's Enzo and Purple Stretchy Pants, by the way. I think you know who's who already, just by looking at them." Carlos said.

"Purple Stretchy Pants? But he's just one giant in purple. He's got no pants on him.." Boon said.

Purple Stretchy Pants approached me. We were both almost the same size because of our huge muscle. Both of us were bursting with muscles and a bad attitude. I could see and feel a lot of that bad attitude directed towards me now.

"That's because my skin is purple, and I'm wearing these custom purple, stretchy pants. It kinda blends well together. You can call me PSP for short, by the way."

"Nice to meet you, PSP."

I stretched out his large hand for PSP to shake. Unfortunately, he did not shake it. Instead, he threw a powerful right hook at me. It felt like getting hit by a giant ten-wheeler truck. Ten times over. I took the full impact of the powerful punch, and went flying across the yard. I landed on several benches smashing them all, in the process. Not the softest landing.

"I also don't like people making fun of my skin and pants." PSP said.

"PSP! You didn't have to do that!" Carlos said.

"Oh but he did, Carlos. He really did. Now, he's going to pay for doing it." I said.

"Guys, I think you just both started out on the wrong foot, and.."

Carlos' words fell on deaf ears. Before he could do anything, I was already up and running towards PSP. I threw myself at PSP and struck him like a missile scoring a direct hit on its target. PSP was caught off-guard by the sudden impact. He never knew that anybody could hit him that hard and he was knocked off of his feet.

PSP was on the ground, and I intended to keep it that way. I started raining down fist after fist on PSP. Each fist was as strong as giant stone hammers and they fell on PSP over and over again.

"Boon! That's enough already, Boon! He can't defend himself! PSP's helpless!" Carlos said.

"Hey! No fighting in the yard!"

Several guards poured into the yard towards me while I was still pounding the snot out of PSP. They all threw themselves at me to try and hold me down. Not so smart. With one powerful flick of both my arms, I tossed the guards aside like water from a dog drying himself.

"Wasn't that the new prisoner Noob? Didn't he spend some time in solitary confinement?" one of the guards asked.

"He sure did, but it changed him into a monster!" the other guard said.

"Maybe he just made the most of his time in solitary. Rush him again!"

The guards all jumped at us again, but it was futile. We were both simply too strong. We swatted away the guards like mammoths swatting away flies. With the guards down, it was only the two of us standing, and no one between us.

"I'm going to get you for that! No one knocks me down like that! No one!"

"And no one punches me like that, while I'm just talking to them!"

We charged at each other like two runaway trains, on opposite ends of the same track. We were both running straight at each other, and no one was sure who would be left standing.

"Stop it already! Both of you! What do you think you're doing? We're not here to argue!" Carlos said.

We both ignored Carlos and charged at each other. We probably would have killed each other, if we didn't hear the sound of gunfire. Two shots rang out. The shots hit both of us, and we stopped suddenly, dead in our tracks. I had a hard time standing up, and it felt as if my legs were made of rubber, or jelly.

"Whoa! What was that? I'm not feeling too good!" PSP said.

"Can't..stay... on... my... feet...!"

"What was that?" Carlos asked.

"It's him! Look!"

Enzo pointed towards a large man walking confidently towards us. It was Warden Mack. Walking beside him was his faithful pet, Mack Jr. The warden also carried a large rifle that seemed massive, even for him. The barrel of the rifle was still smoking, and it was clear that he fired the shots.

"That's two bullets loaded with tranquilizers that could put down 10 elephants each. I figured it would be more than enough stopping power to deal with you two morons!"

We both fell on the floor like two sacks of potatoes. We just couldn't move.

"Take them both to solitary, boys! There's more than enough room there to separate them, even if they are two giants."

The guards had a much easier time taking us now. We were handcuffed and dragged away. It took a while and considerable effort, but they managed to somehow move us. It was only Carlos and Enzo now in the yard, along with the other stunned prisoners.

"What do we do now, Carlos? The warden just took PSP and that new guy away?"

Carlos shook his head.

That was all I saw and heard from Carlos and Enzo after that. I was taken into solitary, and I knew what was going to happen. I could easily tell from the way Carlos and Enzo looked at us, as they dragged me away.

They were both going to complete their jailbreak without me and PSP. In the old days this would have frightened me. I would have wanted to leave this place at all costs. The idea of going back to solitary would have frightened me once.

Now, I felt none of those emotions. I didn't care that they were taking me back to solitary, or that I wouldn't be able to escape with Carlos and Enzo. I didn't need to anymore. With my new strength and body, I could rule this prison and no one would be able to stop me. No, no one could. I will rule this jail. It's going to happen. I used to be afraid, but not anymore. I've changed. They can do anything to me, but it won't stop me. It won't stop BOON.

The End.

Didn't like the ending? Double-back and start over! There are many other endings that may suit your taste!

Entry #12:

Kings of the Roost.

I just took one look at Carlos, and I knew what to decide.

"You're right Hoyce. I don't need this thin and scrawny weakling. I'm a big man now, and I deserve a gang that can run with me, and give me more power. I'm going with the T'recsz!"

"Haha! Good choice, Boon! I knew you would make the right choice! I just knew it!"

Carlos shook his head.

"You're making a big mistake here, Boon. I could have offered you the best thing anyone could get in this place!"

I smirked at Carlos.

"Yeah? What could you possibly offer me that would be worth my time?"

Carlos thought about it for a moment. He wanted to say something, but whatever it was, he kept it to himself.

"Nothing. It's nothing. You've made your choice, after all."

"What a wuss! I knew you were just wasting my time!"

"Don't worry, Boon! I'll introduce you to some real winners tomorrow, during yard time!" Hoyce said.

The rest of the day passed, quietly enough. Yard time came around, and all the prisoners were led outside on the spacious prison yard. It was just about the only time they could step outside and catch some fresh air.

I went outside and immediately caught sight of a prisoner waving frantically at me. I realized that this was Hoyce. He was a lot thinner than I thought he would be, and he looked a lot less intimidating than Carlos. He actually looked a little familiar, like a cross between an MMA guy and a singer. I don't know. And to think he was a member of the toughest prison gang, the T'recsz? I don't know. He looked a bit like a letdown but oh well..

"Boon! Come here big man, and let me introduce you to the boys!"

There were two other men with him, and both looked pretty large and intimidating. Now we were getting somewhere.

"Meet the boys, big man! This here's Lean Meat, and this here's Andro!"

Lean Meat had long hair and a thick moustache and beard to match. He also had a protruding belly which indicated that he was probably in jail for quite some time now. Andro was much younger and appeared more energetic than Lean Meat.

"These guys are the bomb, and they'll be like your soldiers!"

"Soldiers?"

"Heh. Didn't you get my message last night? Our gang needs a leader, and when I saw you come out of solitary confinement, I knew that we had found him! You're our leader man, the one who's going to carry our gang to a new age of power in this jail. We're going to be the kings of this here, roost!"

Now Hoyce was talking. I really liked the sound of being the leader of the entire jail. It was something I could really get used to.

"Heh. Yeah, I think I like the sound of that!"

"Hey! Are you the guy that just walked all over Carlos?"

A large man, almost as large as myself, moved angrily towards me. Carlos tried to stop him, but he would have none of it. He continued to approach me. He would have actually looked pretty intimidating if it wasn't for his ridiculous purple skin.

"Take it easy, PSP! It's all right. We don't need any of this!" Carlos said.

PSP ignored his friend's pleas and continued to walk towards me. He was now in my face. Okay, not good. I did not like that at all.

"You think you're some big shot around here? You think you can just reject my friend's offer like that? Well, let me tell you now, I'm not afraid of you, and I don't appreciate that kind of behavior!"

PSP shoved me with both of his large hands. I actually felt it! This was clearly a challenge, and everyone saw it.

"Whoa! This guy's challenging you! Are you just going to let him do that, Boon?" Hoyce said.

"Yeah! You going to let an Ocular push you around? An Ocular? A member of the lowliest gang in the jail?" Lean Meat said.

I looked at my new gang mates and at PSP who was still glaring at me It was time to decide again, and I had to make the right choice. Or should you? I don't know. It's so hard to think. Why don't you do it for me?

If you think that Boon should accept PSP's challenge and defeat him go to Entry #15 (page 73)!

If you think that PSP's challenge is a waste of time, and just ignore him, go to Entry #16 (page 78)!

Entry #13:

Lucky Thirteen: The Name's BOON!

Okay, so I heard both Carlos and Hoyce's offers. It was the least I could do, right? Still, a man like myself with this new and totally awesome bod, could really do only one thing. There was really just one option for myself considering how strong and powerful I had become.

It was simply to stand alone. I didn't need either of them, or their gangs, to become a force of power in the prison.

"Sorry ladies, but this guy has only one dance partner, and that's himself!"

There was a moment of silence, as both Hoyce and Carlos simply couldn't believe what they had heard.

"What? Shocked? Speechless? You kids go on ahead and do whatever it is you want to do. If there's one thing solitary taught me, it's that you can only count on one person in this jail, and that's me!"

The evening came and went, and when morning arrived, they were all at the yard. This was the only time that the prisoners could enjoy some time outside of their cells to get some fresh air.

With all of the prisoners outside, Warden Mack decided to take a stroll in the yard with his dog Jr and some trusted guards. His yard stroll was more of a statement than anything else, that he was still the man in charge of the entire prison.

Warden Mack surveyed the entire prison yard like a king walking all over his lands.

"All right. Everything's in order, and all the prisoners accounted for?"

"Yes sir, Warden Mack. No trouble here at the yard", one of the guards said.

Warden Mack nodded.

"Good. That's the way things should stay."

His eyes fell on me. Mack tried really hard to hide it, but I knew that look he had in his eyes. It was the look of amazement that they all gave me. That look that said;

"How did he get so freakishly big in solitary? How on Earth did that happen?"

The answer was always the same boys..

Pushups. Lots and lots of pushups.

"Everything good there? **NOOB**?"

All right, baby. That was a big mistake, Warden Mack. I heard the warden's words and my yellow blocky face immediately turned red. I had already warned the warden and anyone who cared to listen not to refer to me by that name. It was a warning only Warden Mack refused to heed. His own pride simply got the better of him, and he had to prove to everyone that he was still more powerful than me. You want it that way? Fine.

"What did you just call me?" Boon said.

"You heard me, NOOB. I called you NOOB!"

I gave out a loud cry that sounded more like a beast than a man's and rushed towards Mack. I would have ran over him, right then and there when something crashed right into me. The object hit me so hard on the chest, that I fell to the ground. It was like getting hit by a train. I looked up and saw the strangest sight.

"Who did this to you? Who did this to you?"

That's right. It was Mack Jr. again. He had stepped in front of me and protected Mack like a loyal dog should. The only thing was, he sounded nothing like a dog. He kept repeating that phrase with a cool and straight voice, almost like some kind of soul singer.

"Who did this to you?"

"That's a cool voice you've got there, boy. Too bad that this time I've got to slap the taste out of your mouth too!"

I picked Mack Jr. up and sent him rolling away like some fuzzy football. I kinda felt bad about that considering Mack Jr was such a cool dog with a suave voice, but I had no choice. And he didn't land that bad, anyway.

Well, either way, I had disposed of Mack's powerful pet. Mack saw what I had done to Mack Jr. and he flew into a rage.

"Mack Jr! What have you done? You're going to pay for that!"

Warden Mack charged towards me. He was full of anger and was hardly thinking straight. Bad move, Warden. I threw a powerful fist that smacked him right in the face. Mack ran right into it, and he was sent flying, just as his dog was.

Everyone in the yard saw it, prisoner and guard alike. They were all stunned into silence. I stood there, triumphant, and took it all in. I savored the attention because I knew what this meant. This was a huge turning point in the jail.

"You all saw that? That was the warden, and his pet pooch! The big, bad warden that you're all so scared of, and I kicked him straight to next week! I think you're all smart enough to know what that means! If not I'll enlighten you!"

Everyone remained silent.

"There's a new big man in the prison, and that's me!"

No one protested. From that day on, the warden lost all his power in the prison, and it eventually turned into chaos. Any sense of law and order in the jail vanished after the warden was humiliated. All the gangs and inmates respected only one man. They called him BOON. You know who that is. Cool ending, by the way. Nice choice. I'm glad you picked right. If you didn't I would have smacked you up, personally. Remember Noob is gone. There is only BOON.

The End.

Didn't like the ending? Double-back and start over! There are many other endings that may suit your taste!

Entry #14:

It's time for a Jailbreak!

"Are you done with that fork?" I asked.

"I'm almost done, Noob! Stop asking me over and over, and just do your job. There's no guard doing the rounds outside?"

I looked around nervously behind our cell door. Yeah, it was me doing lookout, even as Carlos worked on the wall in our cell. There was a huge hole where one of us could barely fit, and the toilet had been moved. Apparently, Carlos had dug his way through a weakened portion of the wall with his fork. He had done this before I came along, and the hole was almost big enough for both of us now. Carlos' plan was a combination of persistence and sheer genius. I have to admit, the man had brains all right. I guess he really did go to High School.

"No one! Just hurry, already! I can't believe that you discovered that hole in the wall before, and that you kept chipping away at it with your fork! That work must have been torturous and agonizing!"

"You're just making it worse Noob, but yeah, it was tough! And what did you want me to do? When I discovered the weak area here on the wall, I realized that this jail isn't exactly brand new! I smuggled some forks to PSP and Enzo, and the plan was set. When I discovered the pipes and tunnels that connect the cells from underground, well, I realized that an escape was actually possible! You just had to really plan ahead, and that's what we all did!"

65

"With PSP's strength, I'm sure he's probably had an easier time digging away than you, or Enzo!"

Carlos smiled, as he continued to chip away at the wall.

"The big man's strong, I'll give him that much. He's not as smart as me though. Every gang needs its brains and brawns, Noob."

"You're a smart guy, Carlos. No one's questioning that. Are you done?"

I heard a chipping sound from the wall. It sounded as if Carlos chipped away a substantial part of the wall. I was a little worried that someone would hear the wall collapse.

"There! I just about got it! The wall's come down, and we can both squeeze through now!"

"Yeah, but it sounded like an earthquake from where I am! Didn't anyone hear that?"

"Just get in that hole, and let's scram, Noob!"

We both raced into the hole Carlos made like two rats entering their hole. We exited the cell, and entered a dark and narrow pipe. It was tough to squeeze in, and crawl through the pipe, but we managed.

"And you say that the plans you stole show where this pipe leads to?" Noob asked.

"Yeah. The pipe connects to PSP and Enzo's cells. It also connects to a pipe system underground. If we follow the pipes we'll exit directly to the joint's front."

"The front of the jail? You mean we won't exit out of the jail directly?" Noob asked.

"Hey, it's the best I could manage. Besides, from there, we just need to get over the wall! That shouldn't be so tough anymore. There's just two guards at best there, and we would have bypassed all the other guards in the entire jail!"

We heard some movement ahead. We came to a fork in the pipe and two familiar figures.

"PSP! Enzo!"

"Great to see you two guys from here! I would hug you both, but as you can see, I'm pretty squeezed in tight right now..." PSP said.

He wasn't kidding. He could barely fit in the pipes, but somehow he did.

"Man, that really looks painful..." Noob said.

"Don't worry, I'll manage. What's important is we get out of here."

"Agreed. Come on guys! Remember the path from the map I had you memorize. Let's get moving."

It was a long crawl, that felt like an eternity for everyone. It was a lot more difficult for poor PSP who was squeezed in so tight. I couldn't bear to watch the large man crawling through the pipe. I was sure that poor PSP was probably going to be sore and red all over after all this was done.

"How are you even crawling through the pipe?" I asked him.

"Don't ask, Noob. I don't know how I'm doing it myself!"

"Hang in there, PSP! We're almost through the pipe! If I remember the map right, we should be above the front of the prison soon!"

"I sure hope so! My butt feels like it's being scraped by a lawnmower here!"

"Ugh! Awful imagery! Did you have to be so specific?" Enzo said.

"Enough already, all of you! We're here!"

Carlos was relieved that we had finally reached the lid above. We all were. The pipe had led to an iron lid, just as the plans of the prison indicated.

"Okay, it should be easy to open enough.." Carlos said.

"Aaand.. I can't open it! It's rusted shut!"

"Great! Now what do we do?" I said.

"Don't worry! Stretchy! Come on and open that lid! You're the only one strong enough here to do it!" Enzo said.

"I don't know if I can. I'm squeezed in this pipe so bad, I feel like a cross between a pretzel and a sardine!"

"You've got to do it, Stretchy! If you don't we're stuck here! Come on!"

PSP took Carlos' words to heart. He had spent enough time in jail. All of them did, and if they were caught, they would never be able to break out. If I got caught here with them, I would never be able to get out at all. Yeah, we all had to leave, right now.

"All right! I'll do it!"

PSP took a deep breath, and pressed his back against the metal lid. He heaved and pushed but it did not budge.

"Darn it! It's rusted shut, tight!"

"Come on, PSP! Put your back into it! We have to get out of here!" Carlos said.

"Don't mean to pressure you, big guy, but he's right. You've got to open that grate!" Enzo said.

"Come on, PSP! You can do it!"

PSP heaved as hard as he could. His face went red, and he put everything he had, and then some. His friends were counting on him. We all were and he could not fail.

The lid popped open. Somehow PSP managed to open it!

"All right! Let's go!"

We climbed out of the lid and saw the prison wall ahead of us. The prison wall was not that high, and there were only two guards, both of whom were walking on faraway opposite ends of the prison. This was the best chance of escape.

"Come on, everyone! Let's make a break for that wall! Once we climb over it, we're free men!"

We all started running for the wall. As the it drew closer, I could already smell the freedom. This was everything we had worked for!

I managed to get to there first. I climbed up to the top of the short wall with ease. I guess I was that desperate to get out of jail. The others were still running towards the wall.

"Boy, I never knew he could run and climb so fast." Enzo said.

"Come on guys! Hurry up!"

It didn't take long for me to spot trouble. The guards had spotted them, and there were several attack dogs right behind them.

"Attack dogs! I knew they would find us!" PSP said.

"Hurry up!"

There was nothing much I could do, but watch from the top of the wall. It was a grim scene. The dogs were fast-gaining on them, and the wall was still some distance away. It appeared as if they wouldn't make it. Unless I did something to distract the dogs.

It's that time again!

If you think that Noob should just jump to the other side and be free go to Entry #17 (page 81)!

If you think that Noob just leave his guys behind, and should try to do something about the dogs, go to Entry #18 (page 83)!

Entry #15:

Boon vs PSP! The Big Showdown!

I could feel the gang's eyes on me. Lean Meat, Hoyce, and Andro were all staring at me, waiting for what I would do next. They were all expecting me to come through here, and I couldn't let them down. There was no way that I was backing down from this giant, purple idiot. I had to show no fear. After all, I was not a noob anymore. I was now Boon, the Big Man!

"I'm not going to let some big purple wuss walk all over me. You just made the biggest mistake of your life."

I threw a powerful punch right at PSP's face. The punch caught him flush on the cheek, and he did not see it coming. PSP went flying across the yard. A loud cheer rose from Hoyce and the others.

"Yeah! That's showing him! No one messes with T'recsz!"

"And no one messes with Boon, the Big Man!"

I smiled and acknowledged their cheers. It felt great to have a gang backing him up like this. Noob never had it this good. If was a huge rush, and I enjoyed it a lot.

"Yeah. I could get used to this."

That was right about the time I was struck by the runaway bullet train that slid off the tracks.

It was PSP, and he charged at me like a cannonball that had just been fired. I never saw it coming and I was knocked to the ground.

PSP was now all over me, landing several powerful blows. I have to say that he was a purple goof ball, but he was a purple goof ball who could hit hard.

"Your punch took me by surprise there, but I'm not letting you do that again!" PSP said.

"All right! That's enough! Break it up! I said break it up!"

It was the warden, his dog, and several prison guards. They were all on top of PSP, and somehow, they managed to pull him away from me. They were greeted by catcalls and protests by the prisoners, but they still somehow managed to pull one big man, away from another.

"Let them fight! Let them fight! Let them fight!"

"Shut up! I'm not going to allow any kind of fighting in my jail! Everyone get back to your cells! As for you two, another five updates in solitary should cool you both down."

"Who did this to you? Who did this to you?"

Warden Mack's dog wasn't barking. He was simply repeating the phrase over and over again to the chants of the inmates. It was a strange way to bark, but Mack Jr. was always a strange dog.

"That is one sick dog." I said.

"Shut up, already! You're going back to solitary for this, Boon! I hope it was worth it." Mack said.

It was another five updates in solitary but I didn't really care. I saw the look on

Hoyce and the others' faces, and they were all very pleased. Yep, I had earned their respect, and I would lead them now. First it was their gang, but I knew that I could take it a lot further than that. Somehow, I would find a way to take down Warden Mack and that crazy dog of his. Once that was over with, the jail was mine. Noob was far gone now. In his place was Boon, the Big Man! Who needs to the jailbreak? I'm happy right here, right now.

"Oh it was worth it, warden. It was really worth it."

The End.

Keep reading to see the other endings you may have missed!

Entry #16:

No Need for Trouble.

"Come on, Boon! What are you waiting for? Hit him already!"

"Yeah, no one insults a T'recsz like that, much less an Ocular!"

"You can't let that stand, man!"

Yeah, I heard my gangmates egging me on. I heard them asking me to kick PSP's butt. They all wanted a big showdown now, including PSP himself. Everyone was looking to see a good old fashioned jail beat down.

Unfortunately, that wasn't going to happen.

"Ain't no one going to be fighting now."

"What?"

Hoyce and the others were all stunned at what they heard. They simply could not believe it. The very reason they allowed me to join was because they saw someone strong, someone who wouldn't back down from a fight. This was simply unbelievable, and unacceptable.

"Are you serious man? You can't just back down from a challenge like that!" Hoyce said.

"I just can't see the point of fighting. You want to fight me PSP, go ahead. But

I warn you, you throw a punch at me, or just poke me the wrong way, and I will defend myself."

I eyed PSP carefully to see if he would bite. I threw down the warning at him, and he could have easily ignored it. If he struck me, I would definitely strike back.

In the end, PSP decided, it simply wasn't worth it.

"You're not worth my time. You're not as tough as you look."

The purple giant walked away from me and my gang. A huge showdown was avoided, but was it the right course of action?

"You just let him go like that, man."

"Yeah, I can't believe you would let an Ocular insult you like that."

Hoyce did not say anything against his fellow gangmates. Something inside him, told him that they had a point.

"Maybe I was wrong to recruit you in the gang, man. Maybe I was really wrong."

The three members of T'recsz walked away from me. I felt the heavy weight of disappointment on my shoulders.

"Guys? Guys?"

They all ignored me and left me there all alone. They didn't say a word, but I heard what they were saying loud and clear. It was the sound of disappointment and rejection. I could have led the gang and taken over the prison. Instead, I backed down from a fight, and now I was all alone and without a gang. I couldn't believe how stupid I was. Life in jail was about to get a whole lot more difficult, and it was all my fault.

The End

I know, I know. That ending wasn't what you wanted, right? Well, try reading the other endings you've missed. Some of them are much better, I promise!

Entry #17:

Honor among thieves.

"Come on! Hurry up guys! The dogs are right behind you!"

I called out to my friends, but I knew that they would not make it. There was simply no way they could outrun the dogs, climb the wall and get to the other side. The dogs were simply faster. It was impossible.

"There's no chance that they're going to get here in time. I better just bail and save myself!"

Yeah, I decided to do the practical thing, and jumped to the other side of the fence. Forget honor. I just wanted to break out of jail.

"Noob!"

"No!"

"The slimy rascal left us behind!"

I heard them calling out to me from the other side. There was also the sound of dogs growling and some men speaking. Yeah, the dogs and the guards had caught up to them, and it was over now. They were caught and I was finally free! That wasn't so hard right?

Wrong.

I jumped down from the wall and savored the smell of fresh air. The suburbs and the city were just a short run from here. I was free and I could finally have my life back!

Nope.

"Hold it right there, inmate."

I turned around and saw a prison guard. He was pointing his gun right at me.

"What..? One more guard? Outside the wall?"

The guard nodded.

"Of course. I'm the guard at the jail entrance. I'm stationed right at the gates. When I heard the commotion, I rushed here knowing you would jump off at this exact spot. I saw everything happen and I have to say, that was a pretty low blow you did back there. No one abandons their friends like that. I always thought there was still honor, even among thieves. But I guess I was wrong."

I had no choice but to put my hands up. I was led back to the jail in no time. There was no way to explain to Carlos and the others what I did. It was simply inexcusable to leave them like that, and they would not be pleased. Not only did my escape attempt fail, but I also managed to make some enemies here. Things were not looking very good for me now. You could say that I actually deserved all of it.

The End.

Yeah, that was anything but a happy ending! You've got to read the other endings to get to the better ones!

Entry #18:

No one gets left behind.

I looked past the wall for only a moment. I could see the suburbs, the city, and all the servers past the jail. I saw the lights of the cars, and the players doing the stuff they usually did in Robloxia. It was all so beautiful, and so attractive from where I was standing.

"The city, the suburbs, everything's so close from here. I can be free again, if I just jump to the other side."

I looked at Carlos, Enzo, and PSP. The dogs were gaining on them, especially on the poor purple giant. PSP had exerted himself too much, opening the rusty lid, and they were gaining on him. Once they tackled him, it would be easy to tackle Enzo and Carlos.

"It would be so easy to just jump to the other side, but I can't! I just can't leave them behind like that!"

I took some stones from the top of the wall. They were numerous, and I began to throw the stones at the dogs. Some stones struck the dogs, and they began whimpered.

"There! Get out!"

"Nice going Noob!" Carlos said.

"You can congratulate me later! Just get up, all of you! Hurry!"

Soon, more dogs took the place of the ones that I had pelted with the stones. The three prisoners had all managed to reach the wall, and were frantically climbing now.

"Stop them!"

It was PSP who was the last to reach the top of the wall. Finally, all three of them made it, and jumped to the other side.

Once the three of them jumped down, a guard from the outside greeted them.

"Hold it! No one move!"

Before he could do anything, a swift blow from PSP knocked him out.

"That takes care of the guard outside, but how are we going to escape now? They're going to be bursting out of that jail any minute!" Noob said.

"Don't worry! I got that covered too!"

Carlos pointed to a nearby parked car. There was a driver inside waiting for us and waving us forward.

"Everyone, get into that car!"

The four of us got inside, and the car sped away.

"Right on time!" the driver said.

"Guys, meet my contact from the outside, Foxbert! Foxbert's the best getaway driver in all of Roblox! He's spent all his life in Vehicle Simulator, so he really knows his craft."

"Nice to meet you, Foxbert! Boy, you really think of everything, don't you, Carlos?"

Enzo and PSP smiled. The big purple giant managed to smile, even as he was again cramped into a small space.

"Get used to it, Noob! You run with Carlos, you'll see that he usually has all the bases covered. The man's a living thinking cap!"

"Yeah? Maybe he could have thought of getting a bigger car! I can barely move here!"

"Hah! Stop complaining, big purple! At least we managed to get away good!"

Carlos smiled at me.

"Yeah, we couldn't have done it without our newest recruit here. Thanks for waiting for us, Noob."

I smiled.

"Don't mention it guys."

I was finally free from the jail. Better than that, I even managed to make three good friends that I could count on in a real pinch. Okay so maybe I was no real criminal multi-tasker, but that didn't matter anymore. What was important was that we were all free, and I had a second chance at life again. Everything was looking up for all of us and we were ready to face anything that would come our way.

The End

Leave a review on Amazon to boast how quickly you got to the correct ending!

Robloxia Kid

11848871R00055

Made in the USA
Lexington, KY
16 October 2018